THE INDUSTRIAL REVOLUTION

Volume 10

The Industrial Revolution and American Society

James R. Arnold & Roberta Wiener

Grolier

An imprint of Scholastic Library Publishing
Danbury, Connecticut

First published in 2005 by Grolier
An imprint of Scholastic Library Publishing
Old Sherman Turnpike
Danbury, Connecticut 06816

For information address the publisher:
Scholastic Library Publishing, Old Sherman Turnpike,
Danbury, Connecticut 06816

Library of Congress Cataloging-in-Publication Data

Arnold, James R.
   The industrial revolution / James R. Arnold and Roberta Wiener.
   p. cm
   Includes bibliographical references and index.
   Contents: v. 1. A turning point in history – v. 2. The industrial
revolution begins – v. 3. The industrial revolution spreads – v. 4. The
industrial revolution comes to America – v. 5. The growth of the
industrial revolution in America – v. 6. The industrial revolution
spreads through Europe – v. 7. The worldwide industrial revolution –
v. 8. America's second industrial revolution – v. 9. The industrial
revolution and the working class v. 10. The industrial revolution and
American society.
   ISBN 0-7172-6031-3 (set)—ISBN 0-7172-6032-1 (v. 1)—
ISBN 0-7172-6033-X (v. 2)—ISBN 0-7172-6034-8 (v. 3)—
ISBN 0-7172-6035-6 (v. 4)—ISBN 0-7172-6036-4 (v. 5)—
ISBN 0-7172-6037-2 (v. 6)—ISBN 0-7172-6038-0 (v. 7)—
ISBN 0-7172-6039-9 (v. 8)—ISBN 0-7172-6040-2 (v. 9)—
ISBN 0-7172-6041-0 (v. 10)
   1. Industrial revolution. 2. Economic history. I. Wiener, Roberta.
II. Title.

HD2321.A73 2005
330.9'034–dc22   2004054243

Printed and bound in China

CONTENTS

INTRODUCTION

By 1870 the Industrial Revolution was more than 100 years old, yet only five countries in the world were industrialized—Great Britain, Belgium, France, Germany, and the United States. These five accounted for more than 80 percent of the world's manufacturing output. Mass production in factories brought about the dramatic increase in these nations' industrial output. A century of industrialization changed the way people worked and the conditions under which they lived.

The first step in the growth of mass production was to gather workers in one place, the factory. Next came various techniques to improve productivity, such as specialization of labor. Rather than assembling a product from beginning to end, individual workers made individual components. They became specialists, doing the same thing day after day. Mass production proved hugely efficient. It brought about great price reductions and thus made more products affordable to larger numbers of consumers. But mass production, the repetitive manufacture of identical items, was mind-numbing work and took place in large, public, and impersonal factories in industrial towns.

Traditional behavior patterns of workers within cottage industries (see Volume 1) had been entirely different from those required in large factories. Home workers formed personal relationships—a handicraft master with his journeyman or a weaver with the spinners who supplied his yarn. Workers frequently came and went as they pleased. While at work they could stop to chat, take longer breaks as the mood struck, and enjoy traditional idle days and holidays. Children mostly worked alongside their parents.

The imposition of factory discipline changed behavior patterns by prohibiting much of what had taken place in the past while creating new social classes in the process. A new class of worker, the

The Blackstone River Valley in New England saw the beginnings of industrial America. By 1828 laborers had finished digging the Blackstone Canal, which allowed industry to boom along the river. Within a few decades the Blackstone Valley from Worcester, Massachusetts, to Pawtucket, Rhode Island, became one of the most densely industrialized regions in America.

foreman, emerged. The foreman's job was to hire and fire workers, and to ensure that the work went according to management's orders. Although most foremen came from the workers' ranks, they were expected to represent management. The presence of foremen meant that factory workers labored under close supervision on a daily basis. This was a marked departure from the past. Personal relations between employers and workers disappeared, along with the daily give-and-take that had once existed in cottage industry and small workshops. The growing social distance between factory owners and workers contributed to increasingly violent conflict over wages and working conditions.

Workers and social reformers alike questioned the harsh living and working conditions imposed by industrialization. Governments weighed the fairness of easing industrial work conditions against the cost to society and businesses. In the United States, as elsewhere, industrialization led to widespread social unrest. Workers organized unions to protest their long hours and low pay, and social reformers campaigned for limits on child labor and improved working and living conditions.

Percentage of World Manufacturing Output in 1870	
Great Britain	31.8
United States	23.3
Germany	13.2
France	10.3
Russia	3.7
Belgium	2.9
Italy	2.4
Canada	1.0
Sweden	0.4
All Others	11.0

WORKING CONDITIONS IN THE UNITED STATES

The Industrial Revolution had brought a new pace of work and a lifetime of supervision and discipline imposed by a separate management class. At the same time, because most factory jobs were extremely specialized, workers derived little sense of achievement from their work.

A TYPICAL FACTORY

The Matteawan Company operated in 1846 at a site near the Hudson River in New York. It consisted of a cotton factory, a

Opposite: A timetable for a Lowell, Massachusetts, textile mill.

Below: A New York factory in 1848.

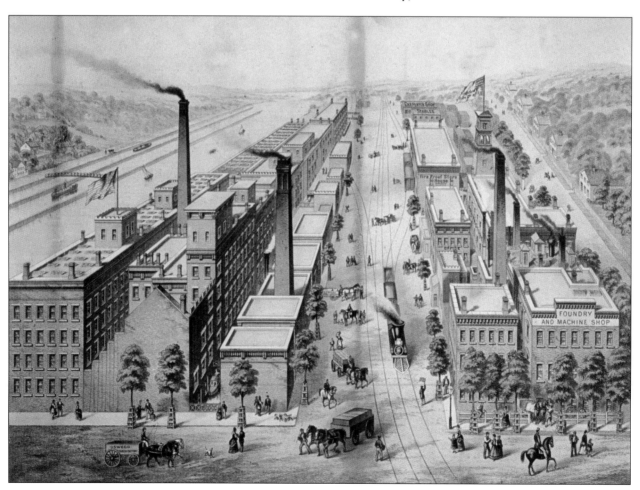

TIME TABLE OF THE LOWELL MILLS,

Arranged to make the working time throughout the year average 11 hours per day.

TO TAKE EFFECT SEPTEMBER 21st., 1853.

The Standard time being that of the meridian of Lowell, as shown by the Regulator Clock of AMOS SANBORN, Post Office Corner, Central Street.

From March 20th to September 19th, inclusive.

COMMENCE WORK, at 6.30 A. M. LEAVE OFF WORK, at 6.30 P. M., except on Saturday Evenings.
BREAKFAST at 6 A. M. DINNER, at 12 M. Commence Work, after dinner, 12.45 P. M.

From September 20th to March 19th, inclusive.

COMMENCE WORK at 7.00 A. M. LEAVE OFF WORK, at 7.00 P. M., except on Saturday Evenings.
BREAKFAST at 6.30 A. M. DINNER, at 12.30 P. M. Commence Work, after dinner, 1.15 P. M.

BELLS.

From March 20th to September 19th, inclusive.

Morning Bells.	*Dinner Bells.*	*Evening Bells.*
First bell,..........4.30 A. M.	Ring out,..............12.00 M.	Ring out,...........6.30 P. M.
Second, 5.30 A. M.; Third, 6.20.	Ring in,...........12.35 P. M.	Except on Saturday Evenings.

From September 20th to March 19th, inclusive.

Morning Bells.	*Dinner Bells.*	*Evening Bells.*
First bell,..........5.00 A. M.	Ring out,...........12.30 P. M.	Ring out at..........7.00 P. M.
Second, 6.00 A. M.; Third, 6.50.	Ring in,.............1.05 P. M.	Except on Saturday Evenings.

SATURDAY EVENING BELLS.

During APRIL, MAY, JUNE, JULY, and AUGUST, Ring Out, at 6.00 P. M.
The remaining Saturday Evenings in the year, ring out as follows :

SEPTEMBER.		NOVEMBER.		JANUARY.	
First Saturday, ring out 6.00 P. M.		Third Saturday ring out 4.00 P. M.		Third Saturday, ring out 4.25 P. M.	
Second " " 5.45 "		Fourth " " 3.55 "		Fourth " " 4.35 "	
Third " " 5.30 "					
Fourth " " 5.20 "		DECEMBER.		FEBRUARY.	
		First Saturday, ring out 3.50 P. M.		First Saturday, ring out 4.45 P. M.	
OCTOBER.		Second " " 3.55 "		Second " " 4.55 "	
First Saturday, ring out 5.05 P. M.		Third " " 3.55 "		Third " " 5.00 "	
Second " " 4.55 "		Fourth " " 4.00 "		Fourth " " 5.10 "	
Third " " 4.45 "		Fifth " " 4.00 "			
Fourth " " 4.35 "				MARCH.	
Fifth " " 4.25 "		JANUARY.		First Saturday, ring out 5.25 P. M.	
NOVEMBER.		First Saturday, ring out 4.10 P. M.		Second " " 5.30 "	
First Saturday, ring out 4.15 P. M.		Second " " 4.15 "		Third " " 5.35 "	
Second " " 4.05 "				Fourth " " 5.45 "	

YARD GATES will be opened at the first stroke of the bells for entering or leaving the Mills.

SPEED GATES commence hoisting three minutes before commencing work.

TENEMENT: a building divided into numerous small apartments, often overcrowded or in poor condition

Opposite and below: A New England factory owner's house and the apartments where the workers lived illustrate the social divide that existed between employers and employees.

card factory, and a machine shop that built machines for those factories and for sale elsewhere. The company employed 300 workers who lived in 100 company-owned **tenements**.

The Matteawan Company made rigid rules for its employees. During working hours it allowed no visitors unless they came for business reasons. When the factory bell rang, all workers had to be at their stations within five minutes. Then all entrances except through the main office to the factory closed. (Imagine the stampede if a fire broke out!) No one could leave work without permission.

The company knew that social activists had begun to complain about factory work conditions. The company responded with the following: "To convince the enemies of domestic manufactures that such establishments are not 'sinks of vice and immorality,' but, on the contrary, nurseries of morality, industry, and intelligence, a strictly moral conduct is required of every one."

The company also worried about its own workers causing problems. So it tried to convince them that management and

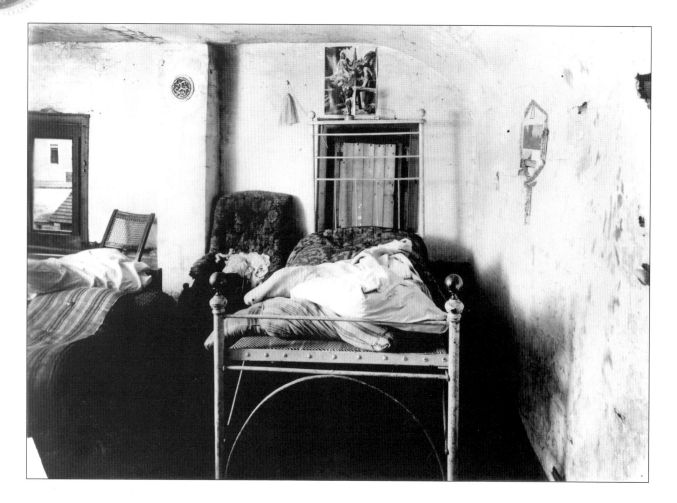

A worker's apartment.

the workers were part of a team by asserting that the company was "desirous of cultivating the most friendly feeling with the workmen...believing they are to rise or fall together."

Regardless of a factory's efforts to convince its workers that owners and workers would "rise or fall together," many American workers knew that this was not so. During times of economic slowdown and in places where the general economy was less robust, the lower classes particularly confronted a difficult combination of low wages, underemployment, poor housing, and despair. Unskilled workers were the hardest hit.

UNSKILLED WORKERS

When mechanization and the factory system first came to the United States, most factory laborers came from the nearby, native born, white population. After the Civil War (1861-65) three trends combined to change that: The number of factory jobs increased faster than the supply of native-born whites; working conditions deteriorated; and because of steam and electric power more new factories were built in cities. As a result, outside of the South, immigrants or nonwhites, particularly women and children, filled most of the unskilled factory jobs.

Newly arrived immigrants had to both learn English and adjust to factory discipline. A typical company booklet to teach reading combined the two objectives. Immigrant workers read aloud:

"I hear the whistle. I must hurry.
I hear the five minute whistle.
It is time to go into the shop.
I take my check [tag] from the gate board and hang it on the department board.
I change my clothes and get ready to work.
The starting whistle blows.
I eat my lunch.
It is forbidden to eat until then."

Workers at spinning machines in a North Carolina cotton mill, 1908.

INDUSTRIAL ACCIDENTS AND DISASTERS

Early factory machines had no protective barriers between workers and rapidly moving parts. If a worker's attention wandered for an instant, a finger or a loose sleeve might get caught in a machine and pull the worker into the machinery. Some workers lost fingers or entire arms, or suffered even worse injuries.

The risks of fire, explosion, or structural failure were ever-present in factories. Industrial fires occurred with grim regularity. The infamous 1911 Triangle Shirtwaist Factory fire in New York killed 146 workers. Heavy machinery and the metal shafts and gearing required to run them led to collapses of mill wall and floor sections. The rapidly turning flywheels at a mill's main power source came loose and caused explosive damage to machinery and buildings. Overworked steam engines resulted in boiler explosions. Many of these accidents killed workers. Worse, entire factory buildings sometimes collapsed, as occurred in 1860 in Lawrence, Massachusetts.

On January 10, 1860, the Pemberton Mill in Lawrence, Massachusetts, suddenly collapsed and burned, trapping hundreds of women workers and killing 88. The investigation uncovered substandard support pillars and other defects in the hastily built factory.

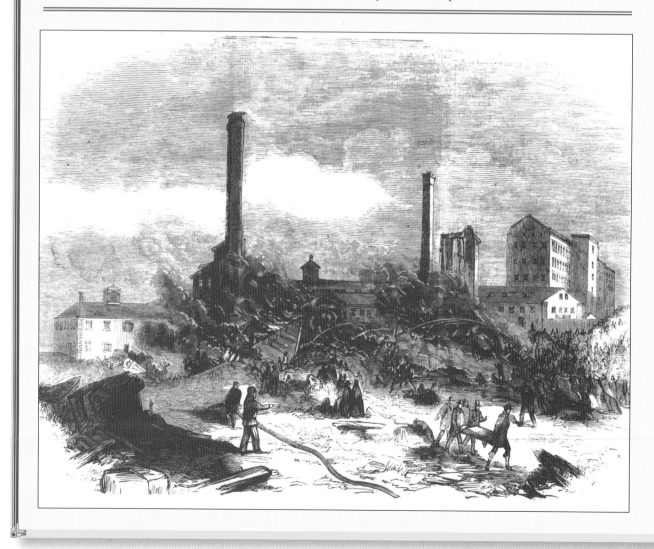

The damage caused by engine explosions in Manchester, New Hampshire, 1891 (above), and Lowell, Massachusetts, 1911 (right). The 1891 explosion of a 30-foot, 68-ton flywheel killed three people and destroyed a building.

Established immigrant groups like the French Canadians and the Irish worked in New England textile mills. Recent immigrants found specialty niches: Jewish women molding cigars in Philadelphia; Polish men butchering cows while Polish women stuffed sausages in Chicago meat-packing plants; Italian men assembling cans in New York. Almost all

Below: An Ohio boy who lost his arm in a factory accident in 1908.

such immigrants hoped to better themselves after a few years of work by either rising up the factory pay scale or by saving enough money to buy land for themselves. They were not always successful.

Factory work remained dirty and dangerous. Exposure to chemicals, dust, and a host of waste byproducts led to serious diseases. Factory machines had few or no safety features, so injuries were common. Neither health insurance nor worker's compensation (to pay the worker while he recovered from an injury) existed. Unskilled workers labored with the knowledge that if they fell sick, got injured, or complained, they could easily be replaced.

Opposite: The air in textile factories was full of lint particles, especially where the raw fibers were processed. Workers at wool-carding machines in Boston, 1912.

Below: Boys working the night shift at an Indiana glass works, 1908.

CHILD LABOR IN THE UNITED STATES

As was the case in Europe, during preindustrial times American children had participated in the cottage industries and in farm work. Parents or older siblings directed young children to do such tasks as carding, sorting, and spinning. In the fields children planted, weeded, and tended crops and animals. The labor children contributed often made a crucial economic difference in how well a family lived.

Parents also apprenticed their children to local craftsmen in hopes that they could learn a trade. Working conditions for apprentices varied depending on the characteristics of the family they served. Many masters treated their apprentices the same way they treated their own children, which is not to say that they treated them well.

Ben Franklin began work as a printer's apprentice at age nine. His master, who happened to be his brother, beat and mistreated him so harshly that he ran away before completing his time. John Fitch, the inventor (see Volume 5), was apprenticed to a clockmaker. The clockmaker's wife boiled up a mutton and bean broth, and served it to Fitch for all his meals for a solid week. Fitch recalled that after he complained, "She found an immediate remedy by adding water."

Many other masters and their wives behaved kindly toward apprentices. Regardless of how masters and parents treated apprentices, both expected children to work hard in the family business at an early age.

CHILDREN UNDERGROUND

Beginning in the 1840s, American industry started to switch from wood fuel to coal. The next three decades witnessed a dramatic increase in coal production. In 1860 American coal miners dug about 20 percent as much coal as was mined in Great Britain. By 1900 United States coal production exceeded that of Great Britain. While coal mining was dangerous work under any circumstances, the United States lagged far behind western Europe in regulating mine safety. A federal study in

Mining accidents:
See also
Volume 3 pages 13–14
Volume 8 pages 14–15

British children underground:
See also
Volume 9 page 29

1907 concluded that the death rate from mine accidents of 3.39 per thousand was three times higher than that of Great Britain and Belgium. Between 1839 and 1914 more than 61,000 people died inside coal mines. Thousands more died unrecorded deaths later in life from lung diseases caused by exposure to coal dust.

By the 1870s coal mines extended so far underground that mine owners installed fans to force fresh air into the working areas. The forced air system required a complex system of barriers and trapdoors. The barriers frequently had to be opened and closed to let through workers and mule-drawn coal trains. Boys as young as seven or eight, called "trapper boys" (because the air was "trapped" behind the barriers), performed that work.

"PICKING THEIR LIVES AWAY"

Outside of the Pennsylvania hard coal, or anthracite, mines another gang of child workers labored above ground. They

A German immigrant "trapper boy," 500 feet underground in a Pennsylvania coal mine. He had been working since the age of nine and had a chronic cough.

CHILDREN AT WORK

American textile mills and coal mines employed children because they could pay them lower wages. Parents permitted their children to work because they desperately needed the money. During the late 1800s several northern states passed laws limiting working hours and night shifts for women and children, but no such laws existed in the southern states.

The first nationwide law regulating employment of children passed in 1916. The act prohibited interstate shipment of any goods manufactured by workers under the age of 14. A group of mill owners fought the law all the way to the Supreme Court and succeeded in having it overturned. A second law was overturned in 1922. Not until 1933 did a national law restricting child labor get passed and remain in force in the United States.

Opposite: Skilled factory workers were proud of their achievements and often posed for portraits holding a symbol of their work. A young weaver posing with a shuttle around 1855.

Below: A boy at work in a Vermont textile mill in 1909.

Child Labor laws:
See also
Volume 9 pages 30, 49, 54, 57–58

were the "breaker boys," children whose job was to pick the slate from the coal. In 1877 a reporter described their labor:

"In a little room in this big black shed...forty boys are picking their lives away. The floor of the room is an inclined plane, and a stream of coal pours constantly in from some unseen place above, crosses the room, and pours out again into

Below right: The breaker facility at a Pennsylvania anthracite mine, 1905.

Below: Breaker boys at work.

some unseen place below. Rough board seats stretch across the room, five or six rows of them, very low and very dirty, and on these the boys sit and separate the slate from the coal as it runs down an inclined plane. They work here, in this little black hole, all day and every day, trying to keep cool in the summer, trying to keep warm in the winter, picking away among the black coals, bending over until their little spines are curved, never saying a word all the live long day...the coal makes such a racket that they cannot hear anything a foot from their ears."

Some 12,000 breaker boys worked in northeastern Pennsylvania in 1880. Most received little or no education and so could neither read nor write. Instead, they were human machines who "know nothing except the difference between coal and slate."

Coal miners, men and boys alike, confronted an enormous obstacle in their efforts to better their lives. Thousands of immigrants arrived in the United States each year, and they were quite willing to do almost any job, no matter how awful the conditions. Because of them miners knew that if they complained too much, the mine owners would simply dismiss them and hire new workers from the ranks of the immigrants. Nonetheless, when a new, national labor union emerged, many coal miners joined.

THE LABOR MOVEMENT IN THE UNITED STATES

JOURNEYMEN: skilled workers who have learned their trade by completing an apprenticeship or other form of training

Colonial settlers had established some European guilds in America. The guilds principally served the interests of their senior members. During the 1800s a variety of **journeymen's** associations arose, and they acted in many ways like labor unions. Such associations were popular; for example, in 1837 some 300,000 journeyman carpenters belonged to local associations, and sometimes they conducted strikes. The strikes were seldom successful because the associations lacked solidarity, or the ability of individuals to act together as one.

Moreover, as the century went on, technical innovations and new machines began to replace skilled journeymen. For example, puddlers working in steel plants stirred vats of molten iron, added chemicals at just the right time, and assessed when the iron was purified sufficiently to be poured. It took several years of work to acquire the experience and knowledge to advance to a more senior position. The introduction of the

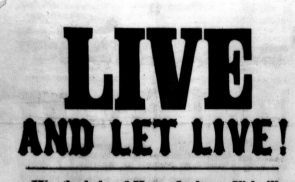

LIVE AND LET LIVE!

We, the help of Hope, Jackson, Fiskville, Arkwright, Harrisville, and Lippitt Mills, have

Resolved, That we will not resume our work in the above mentioned Mills unless our employers will pay us the same wages as we had before the reduction of our wages in 1857; and we hereby solicit the sympathy of all in our cause.

We furthermore request all other operatives not to interfere with our cause by taking our places at lower wages than we now ask for. We believe that the Manufacturers can afford to pay us all that we ask for, as we make nothing but a reasonable demand.

Any one desirous of further information upon this subject, is invited to attend our meetings, the next of which will be holden in the

Harrisville Grove,

On **MONDAY, May 24,** at **10 o'clock, A. M.**

By order of the Committee.

May 21st, 1858.

...n ye that ye beat my people to pieces, ...e faces of the poor? saith the Lord ...---Isa. iii: 15.

Left: New England textile workers who went on strike for higher wages published this poster, which asked people not to take their jobs while they were on strike.

Opposite: Northern factory workers compared their harsh working conditions to those of slaves in the South. This poster publicized the actions of a factory owner when a new law limited the factory workday to 11 hours. The owner locked the factory doors to force his employees to continue working 13-hour days.

THE BEAUTIES OF SLAVERY AT THE NORTH.

In the State of Connecticut, renowned for good morals and steady habits, and in the town of Plainfield, situated on the eastern border of the State, runs that beautiful stream which yet bears its original Indian name of Moosup, which winds through one of the most fertile valleys of the Sate. On this stream are situated eleven Cotton Mills and one large Woolen Establishment, which furnish labor for a large number of poor laboring people who have located there to earn an honest living for their families, under the good and wholesome laws of the State, the Legislature of which has seen fit, in their wisdom, to establish a statute law regulating the hours of labor, in Manufacturing Establishments, at eleven hours and a half per day.

It appears that the Proprietors of all the Mills on the stream have complied with the laws of the State, with the exception one, who has bid defiance to all law and common usage on the stream, and has run his Mills, four in number, thirteen hours per day, of which his poor laborers had the independence to complain, claiming the protection of the Statute Law of the State and left work at the expiration of the lawful hours of labor; but with what result I blush to chronicle. This great and mighty man, at the hour of stopping the Mill, appeared and locked the doors of the Mills, with the help in the Mills, and stationed himself at one door and his son at the other, (not like Sampson of old, with the jaw-bone of an ass,) but with clubs in their hands, to prevent the poor laborers from leaving when they had worked lawful hours, giving strict orders to his overseers to knock down the first child that should attempt to leave the Mill.

This is Northern Slavery; but does it end here? With shame I answer, no! the vile hand of the oppressor and the golden-shod foot of the tyrant are placed on the helpless widow and poor fatherless children. A poor widow, with four small children, is insulted and threatened with being thrown into the street, without the means to procure one days food for her family, and must have suffered had not the help from another Mill, through pity, furnished her with the necessaries of life.

Now, I ask, will not the frowns of an angry God, who has said in His word that He would be the widow's God and a Father to the fatherless, rest upon this fiend in human shape? Ought not the finger of scorn to be pointed at him as he rolls through the street, boasting of his ill-gotten gold?

When we see slavery established in our midst by those who have expressed themselves in the most bitter invectives against the Southern slaveholder, we are led to exclaim, Oh shame where is thy blush, and oh, my country, to what infamy hast thou fallen.

☞ **Please circulate this.**

Bessemer process (see Volume 7) substituted high heat for stirring and made the puddler's art obsolete. Likewise, a journeyman carpenter spent years learning from a master carpenter how to cut, carve, and join wood. In woodworking factories child laborers operated borers, compound carvers, joiners, and power sanders to mass-produce the products that had once been made by hand.

Traditionally, journeymen expected to improve their living standards as they acquired more skills and imagined that eventually they would become masters themselves. The Industrial Revolution shattered that expectation. Some skilled factory positions existed, however, because certain innovations had created new jobs. For example, a federal report in 1911 noted that a pit crane operator in charge of moving steel ingots into the rolling and cutting machinery needed "considerable skill to charge and draw ingots with the rapidity and accuracy required." Nevertheless, most factory workers required less training, strength, and judgment than had been the case in earlier times, so most new jobs were open to a larger set of laborers, including immigrants.

Before the Industrial Revolution, when workplaces were small and people knew one another, an individual worker could discuss issues with his employer and resolve problems personally. The development of large factories and businesses, where midlevel and higher management did not even know their workers' names, made it nearly impossible for individual workers to negotiate with management. Workers concluded that they needed to unite in order to negotiate.

In addition, factors outside of the workers' control caused them immense economic suffering. Throughout the industrialized world railroad construction had provided powerful stimulus to national economies. The railroads also caused sudden economic tailspins as witnessed by the so-called "Railroad Panics" that occurred in the United States in 1857, 1873, and 1893 and in most other industrialized nations at various other times. The panics occurred because capitalists had gone into debt to pay for railroad construction. The railroads expanded too quickly and created excess capacity, so freight rates declined, and the capitalists did not have the profits that they had planned to use to pay off their debts. Instead, they defaulted, and their failure to pay off their loans caused the national economy to plummet.

The railroad panics were one source of economic downturn, but there were many others causes. Regardless of the reason, when demand for goods slowed, factory owners reduced production and laid off workers. Such economic cycles hit the

Opposite: Machines in factories took over the work that had one been done by hand.

poorest workers the hardest, providing one more reason for workers to band together to protect themselves against what they viewed as unfair economic conditions.

THE FIRST UNIONS

By the 1830s a number of unions had organized in the United States, but they tended to be local rather than regional or national, and most did not last long. Many workers concluded that the only way to convince large corporations to negotiate was to form a national union. Only a national union would have sufficient power through the threat and practice of demonstrations, work stoppages, and strikes to negotiate with giant corporations that operated on a national level.

In 1866 William Sylvis, the founder of the Iron Molders' International Union, established the National Labor Union. This national organization tried to merge all local unions into one large group in order to push for reforms such as limiting work to an eight-hour day and creating worker cooperatives to compete with giant corporations. Sylvis thought that the union had its best chance to bring about reforms by entering politics, and so the National Labor Union gave birth to the National Labor Reform Party. Sylvis ran for president of the United States in 1868, failed miserably, and died in 1870. During the subsequent elections of 1872 the party again failed to attract voter support. The economic downturn caused by the following year's railroad panic caused the final collapse of the National Labor Union.

Terence Powderly (below center), the leader of the Knights of Labor, made the strategic mistake of trying to form worker cooperatives to compete with industrial corporations.

FRANK LESLIE'S ILLUSTRATED NEWSPAPER

NEW YORK—FOR THE WEEK ENDING OCTOBER 16, 1886.

No. 1,621.—Vol. LXIII.] [Price, 10 Cents.

GENERAL FITZHUGH LEE. FRANK J. FARRELL, COLORED DELEGATE

VIRGINIA.—TENTH ANNUAL CONVENTION OF THE KNIGHTS OF LABOR AT RICHMOND—FRANK J. FARRELL, COLORED DELEGATE OF DISTRICT ASSEMBLY NO. 49, INTRODUCING GENERAL MASTER WORKMAN POWDERLY TO THE CONVENTION.
FROM A SKETCH BY JOSEPH BECKER.—SEE PAGE 124.

THE KNIGHTS OF LABOR

The Knights of Labor had considerably more success. Formed in 1869, the union steadily grew. Under the leadership of Terence Powderly it

Jay Gould (1836–1892) came from a poor background and spent his early life working as a clerk and a blacksmith, among other jobs. He saved money and bought railroad stock, until he gained control of a major railroad. He earned the label of "robber baron" by engaging in illegal trading on such a large scale that he caused at least one national economic panic and played a role in another. He was able to keep manipulating stocks with impunity because the government had not yet figured out how to prohibit his activities. Gould gained control of several more railroads, as well as the Western Union Telegraph Company, and amassed a fortune of more than $72 million.

RADICAL: extreme; holding extreme views; one who favors major changes to the social order

opened its ranks to both skilled and unskilled workers. Powderly believed that skilled workers had an obligation to help unskilled workers organize unions. A successful strike against the Wabash Railroad in 1885 caused membership in the Knights of Labor to soar to 700,000.

Powderly and the Knights of Labor opposed industrial capitalism. An officer in the union explained, "Our Order contemplates a **radical** change in the existing industrial system. …The attitude of our Order to the existing industrial system is necessarily one of war." Among Powderly's goals were equal pay for women, an income tax (so the wealthy would have to pay more to the government, and the government, in turn, could provide more benefits for the less wealthy workers), and the establishment of worker cooperatives. Powderly wanted "to make each man his own employer." He intended the cooperatives to compete directly with large companies and for the workers to share the profits. His scheme failed, with the cooperatives losing money and bringing ridicule to union members.

More disastrously, the Knights of Labor directly confronted management in several major strikes. In 1886 the union organized a strike against Jay Gould's Southwestern Railroad. The work stoppages failed dramatically. In addition, Powderly declined to support the demand for an eight-hour workday. Consequently, his union slowly lost membership, particularly to a new organization called the American Federation of Labor.

The Knights of Labor is best remembered for two negative accomplishments: Never again would a union try to produce goods in competition with corporations, and several generations would pass before a union again tried to recruit both skilled and unskilled workers.

PROTESTS, STRIKES, AND VIOLENCE

Strikes conducted by the Knights of Labor had failed because striking unskilled workers had been easily replaced by other unskilled workers eager to have a job of any sort. Having seen the problems caused by combining skilled and unskilled workers into the same union, a British-born union organizer, Samuel Gompers, decided to take a different approach.

THE RISE OF SAMUEL GOMPERS

Gompers had immigrated to America in 1863 at the age of 13 to work as a cigar roller. He soon joined the Cigarmakers' International Union. The young Gompers showed real talent as a labor organizer and rose within the union. He ignored the

Samuel Gompers was the most influential union leader in American history. Under his leadership the American Federation of Labor became the nation's most powerful union.

plight of child laborers, women, and unskilled workers, and instead worked exclusively to organize skilled workers into craft unions. Gompers believed that only skilled workers held leverage in any dispute with management. The result was the formation in 1886 of the American Federation of Labor (AFL), which originally consisted of 13 craft unions, including the Cigarmakers' International.

Unlike the situation in Europe, where most labor organizers worked to replace **capitalism** with **socialism**, Gompers understood that American workers simply wanted a better form of capitalism. Toward that goal Gompers promoted economic rights—the right to unionize, work in a safe environment, earn a living wage, and work reasonable hours. Gompers kept the AFL out of any direct involvement in politics. Under his leadership the AFL seldom organized strikes; but when it did, it won. As a result, membership rose steadily from 297,000 in 1897 to 1,676,000 in 1904.

The type of economic rights the AFL promoted appeared reasonable to many Americans. In addition, technological advances in the printing industry combined with a new movement in journalism to influence many opinions regarding workers' rights.

Muckrakers and Robber Barons

Between the fifteenth century, when Johannes Gutenberg's innovations led to letterpress printing (a method of printing with moveable type), and 1810 printing technology changed very little. In 1810 came the first cylinder press, which increased productivity by about 400 percent. In 1846 an American inventor, Richard Hoe, designed the rotary press in which a large cylinder held the type, and several smaller cylinders brought it into contact with sheets of paper. Hoe's invention provided the basis for modern, mass-production newspaper printing. Twenty-one years later, in 1865, William Bullock invented the first rotary web press, which allowed printing on both sides of the paper.

New printing technologies brought more and cheaper books, magazines, and newspapers to a much wider audience. Then as now, sensational writing sold. Among the writers to take advantage were the "muckrakers." In the 1880s and 1890s muckraking journalists (Theodore Roosevelt coined the term "muckraker," by which he meant that writers who exaggerated the facts in order to produce sensational stories were "wallowing in the mud") began publishing strong criticisms of the new industrial economy and the influence of superrich businessmen.

CAPITALISM: the economic system in which property and businesses are privately owned and operated for personal profit

SOCIALISM: an economic system in which the community owns all property and operates all businesses with the aim of sharing the work and profits equally; communists viewed socialism as an intermediate stage in the evolution from capitalism to communism

Opposite top: The means of production became concentrated in fewer and fewer hands as the new industrial order created a small class of capitalists far wealthier and more powerful than the merchants and land owners of previous times. American newspapers were fascinated with the activities of the superrich. J.P. Morgan, the most influential banker of his time, hitting a persistent photographer with his cane.

Opposite bottom: The most advanced printing press of its time on display at the 1876 Philadelphia Centennial Exposition.

Right: Edward Harriman (1848–1909) started his career as an office boy but went on to gain control of much of the American railroad industry. In 1906 his attempts to take over even more of the industry inspired a newspaper cartoonist to portray him as a pirate.

FIXED COSTS: the cost of the buildings and permanent equipment needed to operate a business

Industrialists needed to invest more money than ever before to build large, modern factories. In economic terms larger buildings and more complex machines increased the **fixed costs**. Only the wealthiest could afford high fixed costs. Gradually, a small group of individuals and their companies began to dominate industry. This trend alarmed some people, who worried that the new industrial economy controlled by the superrich represented a fundamental threat to democracy and individual freedom. Muckraking journalists began labeling these men "robber barons." (During the Dark Ages minor noblemen built castles overlooking river crossings or mountain

ON STRIKE

The U.S. government sided with business owners during many of America's earliest strikes. Violence erupted as strikers confronted private guards, local police, National Guardsmen, or federal troops. The public lost sympathy for strikers when radicals among them went too far, as when they tossed a bomb at the Chicago police in 1886. On the other hand, excessive force on the part of police or soldiers turned public opinion against the owners.

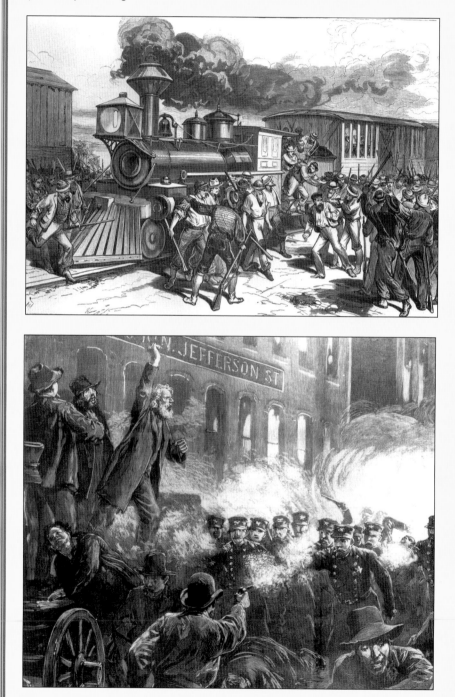

Top: Business was suffering during an economic downturn, so the management of the Baltimore & Ohio Railroad passed some of the burden on to its employees and cut wages by 10 percent. The strike that became known as the Great Railroad Strike of 1877 began in West Virginia. The president of the United States called out federal troops to try to get the railroad running again, and in the resulting fight soldiers shot nine strikers. The strike then spread to four major cities, and troops killed 26 more strikers. One of the many instances of violence in the strike of 1877.

Bottom: During the 1886 strike against the McCormick Reaper Works of Chicago police shot and killed several strikers. A local group of radicals held a meeting at Haymarket Square to protest the killings. When police arrived to break up the meeting, someone threw a bomb into their midst, killing seven officers and injuring 27 others. Although the actual bomb-thrower was never identified, four men were executed for the killings.

Labor unrest:
See also
Volume 9 pages 48, 53

Above: In January 1912 the American Woolen Company of Lawrence, Massachusetts, announced that wages would be cut because a new law reduced the work week from 56 to 54 hours. The strike turned violent, strikers wrecked factory machinery, and a woman striker was murdered. Martial law was imposed as 23,000 workers joined the strike, shutting down the mills. National guardsmen aiming their weapons at strikers.

Below: As the strike against the American Woolen Company continued through the winter, desperate parents, deprived of their earnings, started sending their cold and hungry children to be fed and sheltered by sympathetic people in other towns. The troops beat and arrested women and children at the Lawrence train station to prevent them from doing so. This brutal action caused an international outcry in support of the strikers. After 63 days the owner gave in and agreed to raise wages.

passes and extracted tolls from all who passed by. They were the first to become known as "robber barons.") While the muckrakers attacked the robber barons in print, in workplaces throughout the nation striking unions confronted the robber barons more directly.

THE BATTLE OF HOMESTEAD

In 1892 some 12,000 people lived in the town of Homestead, Pennsylvania. Andrew Carnegie's steel mill employed 3,800 of them. Fewer than one-quarter of Carnegie's employees belonged to the Amalgamated Association of Iron, Steel, and Tin Workers, but Carnegie disliked the union intensely and decided to break it. Carnegie gutlessly wanted to avoid negative public reaction against him personally, including being labeled a robber baron, and so he assigned the job to his trusted lieutenant, Henry C. Frick.

Frick barricaded the mill with barbed wire, set up searchlights, and hired 300 armed detectives belonging to the Pinkerton Agency to guard the barricades. Armed and ready, Frick cut wages 20 percent and hired strikebreakers (workers to replace those who went on strike). As he expected, the Amalgamated Association of Iron, Steel, and Tin Workers went out on strike. An initial skirmish between the strikers and the Pinkerton men left 12 men dead.

The governor of Pennsylvania called in the state militia to restore order. A Russian anarchist (a member of a fringe political movement that wanted to overthrow established governments) attacked Frick in his office and nearly stabbed him to death. That proved the crucial turning point: Until the attack the public sided with the union; after, the public concluded that the union was a dangerous menace.

After five months the union called off the strike. Workers accepted their pay cuts and returned to their 12-hour days. Because the Homestead strike had involved one of the nation's best-known and wealthiest men, it attracted a great deal of attention. In the public view Carnegie emerged as a classic robber baron, selfish and crass. Nonetheless, the affair was a clear demonstration of the power of big businesses to use unfair practices to obtain their goals and to receive support from state government.

THE PULLMAN STRIKE

During the Industrial Revolution no American conflict between labor and management exceeded the importance of the Pullman Strike of 1894.

George C. Pullman had been designing railroad sleeping cars

Opposite: Striking steelworkers confront the Pinkerton guards at Homestead, Pennsylvania.

"MOTHER JONES"

Born in Ireland in 1830, Mary Harris Jones eventually moved to Memphis, Tennessee. She married, had four children, and worked as a school teacher and dressmaker. In 1867 a yellow fever epidemic killed her husband and children. She tried to rebuild her life in Chicago but lost her home in the great Chicago fire of 1871. Given shelter by a local office of the Knights of Labor, she became aware of union issues. She marched on the picket line in the railroad strike in 1877 and was among those attacked by strike-breaking bullies and federal troops.

Jones became an organizer for the United Mine Workers of America in the early 1890s. A miner recalled, "She came into the mine one day and talked to us in our workplace....How she got in I don't know; probably just walked in and defied anyone to stop her." At a mass meeting: "Her voice was low and pleasant, with great carrying power. She didn't become shrill when she got excited; instead her voice dropped in pitch and the intensity of it became something you could almost feel physically." Her life experiences made her ever more determined and radical on behalf of workers rights. In 1905 she helped found the Industrial Workers of the World and thereafter became well known for her involvement in many of the nation's most publicized strikes. The workers who followed her affectionately called her "Mother Jones." She was planning a new series of labor actions when she died in 1930 at the age of 100.

"Mother" Jones, a United Mine Workers organizer, told mine workers to "Pray for the dead and fight like hell for the living!" Her reputation brought her the opportunity to meet U.S. President Calvin Coolidge in 1924.

since about 1855. When train travel boomed after the Civil War, he founded a company that specialized in building luxury coaches as well as dining cars. Pullman became rich from his efforts and in 1881 built a factory town, Pullman, Illinois, outside of Chicago. He exploited his workers terribly, paying low wages in something he called Pullman **scrip**, while his workers lived in a company town where they rented company-owned housing and used the Pullman scrip to purchase overpriced food and clothing from company stores. The Railroad Panic of 1893 caused a national depression. Pullman responded in characteristic fashion by slashing wages while maintaining high rents and company store prices.

Eugene V. Debs, the leader of the American Railway Union (ARU), sym-pathized with the Pullman workers. He also saw a

Above: George Pullman quit school at the age of 14 and became an apprentice cabinetmaker. He eventually turned his skills to the task of remodeling railroad sleeping cars.

SCRIP: pieces of paper used in place of money

Left: National Guardsmen firing at the Pullman strikers

39

splendid opportunity to promote his union. Debs announced that the ARU would not work on any trains that hauled Pullman cars. The boycott brought rail traffic in the Midwest to a standstill, striking a heavy blow against businessmen and merchants who depended on rail traffic. They appealed to the federal government.

President Grover Cleveland and his attorney general supported the businessmen. The government cited the fact that the trains hauled the U.S. mail, and interfering with the mail was a crime, in order to secure a federal court injunction (a type of legal order) outlawing the strike. Debs and his union refused to yield, so Cleveland ordered some 2,000 federal troops to go to Chicago and enforce the injunction. Violence ensued, leaving 12 workers dead, and the government squashed the strike.

Debs went to prison on the charge of contempt of court and conspiring to block the U.S. mail. The American Railway Union collapsed. Pullman, with his reputation in tatters, died a broken man three years later. On the other side the Pullman strike gave corporate leaders a tool, the court injunction, to require labor unions to end strikes and the confidence that federal troops could be called to crush the strikers if the unions refused to return to work. Not until 1932 were labor leaders able to persuade Congress that injunctions were an unacceptable use of government power.

Top: Armed deputies attempting to get a train moving during the Pullman strike.

Right: The Pullman strikers setting up a blockade of rail traffic in Chicago.

EUGENE DEBS

Above left: Eugene Debs's life experiences convinced him that only socialism could provide fairly for working people. Debs leaving prison in 1921

Born in Indiana in 1855, Eugene V. Debs left school as a young teenager to work as a locomotive fireman. He saw firsthand the exploitation of labor by railroad management, and that led him to become involved with labor organizations. At age 20 he began full-time work as a union organizer for the Brotherhood of Locomotive Firemen. He also entered local politics and was elected to the position of city clerk of Terre Haute, Indiana, in 1880. Debs then served in the state legislature but abandoned that path when he decided that the body was too conservative to address the struggle between labor and management.

In contrast to Samuel Gompers, Debs believed that the railroad craft unions needed to include unskilled workers. Accordingly, he established the American Railway Union in 1893 and opened it to both skilled and unskilled laborers. Debs chose to side with striking workers at the Pullman Company by ordering his union to refuse to work on trains that hauled Pullman cars. He then refused a court injunction ordering him to end the strike. He served six months in jail for criminal conspiracy.

World socialism:
See also
Volume 6 pages 62–63
Volume 9 pages 35, 48–49, 59–61

Above: Many socialists objected to America's participation in World War I, arguing that it was a fight among corrupt capitalist powers. However, few Americans shared their view. Soldiers and sailors destroying a socialist banner during a socialist antiwar demonstration in Boston, 1918.

On his release Debs declared himself a socialist, arguing that only the government would manage the railroads and other industries in a way that was fair to working people. His political view put him outside of the established parties, so he helped found the Socialist Party of America. He ran in four consecutive presidential elections beginning in 1900 and in 1912 won about six percent of the vote, by far the highest total for a socialist candidate in American history.

Jailed again in 1917 for his opposition to America's involvement in World War I, he ran for president from his prison cell and received 3.5 percent of the vote. Paroled in 1921, Debs spent the remainder of his life promoting socialism through speeches and writings. Historians regard Debs as the nation's "most influential socialist and critic of the Industrial Revolution." He died in 1926.

THE URBANIZATION OF AMERICA

In preindustrial society worldwide most people lived in rural areas. Trade in agricultural goods far exceeded trade in manufactured ones. Most wealth derived from control or ownership of land. The Industrial Revolution reversed those patterns, and cities came to dominate industrialized society.

Chicago grew into a major junction for shipments crossing the country. Lumber awaiting shipment in Chicago, 1883.

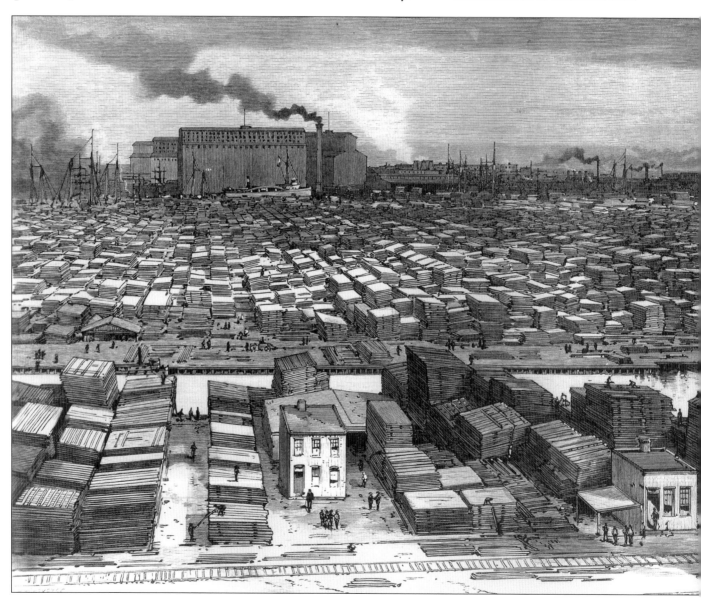

Completed in 1883, the Brooklyn Bridge physically joined Brooklyn and Manhattan Island. It had enormous symbolic importance by demonstrating the promise of technology with its trend-setting use of woven wire rope for its suspension system. Paintings, plays, poems, and later movies, all prominently featured the Brooklyn Bridge.

The statistics of population growth demonstrated the urbanization of the United States. In 1840 the population of major eastern cities almost doubled, while new cities in the Midwest such as Chicago, Cincinnati, and St. Louis began to expand rapidly. The growth of cities accelerated, so that by 1860 nine cities had populations over 100,000: Boston, New York, Brooklyn (not yet connected by bridge with New York), Philadelphia, Baltimore, New Orleans, Chicago, Cincinnati, and St. Louis. The fact that all nine were port cities had contributed greatly to their growth. But that was just the beginning of American urbanization. Fifty years later 50 cities had populations exceeding 100,000 people.

In 1870, 54 percent of Americans worked in agriculture and lived in rural places. By 1910 the number had declined to about 33 percent. On an individual human level the transition from rural to urban life could take place slowly or quite abruptly. For example, a Lowell mill girl who left the family farm to work might marry and raise her family in a factory town. Her daughter could move to Boston to earn her way and end up raising her own family of urban dwellers whose entire knowledge and experience came from their urban environment. In other words, over multiple generations families lost touch with the land and became city people. Alternatively, a Swiss emigrant could leave his alpine flock and two months later begin working in New York's garment industry. That was the typical, and startling, abrupt transition experienced by tens of thousands of European immigrants during the later decades of the nineteenth century.

Wealth and political power followed the path of the population. The great industrialists such as John D. Rockefeller, J.P. Morgan, and Andrew Carnegie managed their affairs from urban headquarters. The largest, most influential banks were in cities. Where there was money, there also was political power. Whereas the Founding Fathers, the leaders who established an independent United States, had included a representative mix of planters and merchants, to an increasing extent the most influential political leaders after the Civil War represented urban interests. Urbanization, brought about by the Industrial Revolution, was a fundamental change in the nature of American society.

THE CHALLENGE OF URBANIZATION

Larger, more densely populated cities presented a host of new challenges. Throughout history getting clean water to urban

People living in cities found work at such places as the American Woolen Company factory in Boston (opposite), shown here in 1912. Many of those who lived in remote rural areas continued to produce textiles at home. This rural North Carolina family (below) was spinning yarn by hand in 1917

dwellers had been a technical challenge. The Romans had built long aqueducts that were engineering marvels to bring water from the country to the city. During the Industrial Revolution many cities had lower-quality water than had Roman citizens. Among many examples, a waterborne epidemic of yellow fever struck Philadelphia in 1793, killing one in every twelve inhabitants.

The solution was a municipal waterworks. In 1799 Philadelphia began construction of a system using two large, low-pressure, Watt-style steam engines to lift water from the Schuylkill River to a city reservoir. A system of wooden pipes carried the water to paying users as well as to free hydrants for the poor. High fuel costs for the steam engines and leaky hydrants combined to make the system unprofitable. Even using more efficient high-pressure engines designed by Oliver Evans failed to reduce fuel costs, while replacing the leaking wooden pipes with iron pipes was too expensive. Finally, by 1823 a new system was in place, created by damming the river and pumping the water with large water wheels. Although Philadelphia's population doubled between 1820 and 1830, the Schuylkill Waterworks provided enough water to keep up with increasing demand.

Not all cities enjoyed a nearby water source. Cities like Boston and New York had to obtain their water from much farther away and at greater cost. A booming new city called Los Angeles set off a water war when it bought up all the water rights in an entire agricultural valley and piped the water to the city for its exclusive use. Likewise, San Francisco built an extensive waterworks (and destroyed vast areas of natural environment in the process) to obtain water from the distant Sierra Nevada Mountains.

Before the introduction of indoor plumbing, flush toilets, cesspools, and sewer systems, city dwellers dumped human waste from their chamber pots into the streets.

Cities and towns with factories grew rapidly. Manchester, New Hampshire, in 1876, had textile factories lining the banks of the Merrimack River.

But providing ample, inexpensive water created a new problem. The new waterworks caused individual water use to rise from 2-3 to 50-100 gallons per day. That increase, coupled with booming populations that produced human waste, overwhelmed a city's ability to handle wastewater.

In addition, around the 1830s a British invention, the water closet (a bathroom with a flush toilet), began appearing in the

homes of the middle and upper classes. In the past city dwellers had deposited their wastes in pits or cesspools. Such pits and cesspools could not accommodate the large volumes of water from the new water closets. As a result, city engineers confronted an enormous sanitation and pollution problem that was probably worse than the original problem before waterworks began delivering public water.

In 1857 Brooklyn, New York, became the first city in the United States to combine storm and wastewater sewer systems. Such systems became standard practice. They made cities

By 1860 America's largest cities had all built waterworks. The Philadelphia waterworks around 1856.

cleaner by carrying away wastes and pollutants and dumping them in rivers, lakes, or the nearby ocean. As time passed, the environmental consequences of that approach became apparent.

An upriver city dumped its untreated wastes into the open water. A city downstream drew its drinking water from the same river. The downstream city had to pay the expense of treating its water or face devastating diseases such as typhoid and cholera. Massachusetts was the first state to address that problem by creating a state board of health in 1867. Other states followed, and soon many boards of health were prohibiting the dumping of raw sewage into waterways. In addition, water-filtering methods helped improve water quality. By 1900 about 28 percent of all city dwellers drank water that had gone through a municipal filtering system. That was enough to significantly reduce the rate of typhoid infection.

Urbanization in Great Britain:
See also
Volume 9 pages 36–41

Although motor vehicles were coming into use, horses still pulled wagons through city streets, such as this Chicago street, in 1915, adding to the unsanitary conditions in urban areas.

Increasing volumes of solid waste presented a different sanitation problem. During the early decades of the Industrial Revolution pigs had routinely wandered the streets of national capitals like London, Paris, or Washington because they usefully ate solid garbage. Likewise, private garbage collectors hauled household garbage to the city's edge to feed pigs that later became food for humans. Garbage collection was haphazard, unregulated—for example, Cleveland had no provisions to collect household garbage until the late 1880s—and consequently an appalling source of contagious diseases. In addition, daily horse traffic into and through the cities contributed another source of filth. By the end of the century a coalition of sanitary engineers, doctors, women's clubs, and concerned businessmen had started the long fight against urban pollution.

The New York City public transportation system included both elevated and subway trains.

URBAN TRANSPORTATION

Many workers lived too far from their places of employment to walk to work. Whether they were factory laborers living in slums or merchants and businessmen living in the suburbs, they needed to move quickly and cheaply. An editorial in an 1872 San Francisco publication stated, "There is at this time no more important question demanding solution from our inventors and mechanics, than that of cheap transit for the

New York City officials
inspecting a new subway car.

clerk, artisan and merchant from the ship or place of business
to the dwelling." This need launched the era of mass
transportation. Engineers built a variety of approaches
beginning with horse-drawn streetcars and eventually
replacing horses with electric power. To avoid congested
streets, they built elevated railways and underground subways.
When the New York City subway opened in 1904, a social
commentator proclaimed, "The event begins the emancipation
of the larger part of the city's population from an excessively
cramped and uncomfortable manner of living."

BIG BUSINESS AND BIG GOVERNMENT

THE RISE OF BIG BUSINESS

After the end of the Civil War in 1865 the national economy continued to expand, creating more opportunities for successful entrepreneurs to sell products. The most successful gained an increasing share of the market and earned greater profits. They outcompeted their rivals, either driving them out of business or engulfing them. Small companies gave way to

As people saved more money, they deposited it in banks for safekeeping. Banks, in turn, loaned money to capitalists to invest in business. New U.S. currency, minted in Washington, D.C., in 1907.

larger companies. A corporate attorney for a large company boasted that the rise of big business could not be resisted: "You might as well endeavor to stay the formation of clouds, the falling of rains, the flowing of streams, as to attempt...to prevent the organization of industry."

Men like Andrew Carnegie and John D. Rockefeller used their business skills to become fabulously rich. Rockefeller developed a legal device called the trust that allowed him to crush rivals, fix prices, and eventually control the oil industry. Industrialists in other sectors utilized the same practices to dominate their fields. In 1890 an attorney for the U.S. Justice Department wrote, "Trusts are becoming as common in industry as furnaces and smokestacks...they are as powerful as any emperor or potentate in the world." One consequence of the rise of big business was an immense concentration of wealth and power in the hands of a few individuals.

THE RISE OF BIG AGRICULTURE

Just as small manufacturing companies found great difficulty competing with larger companies, so it was for small farmers. The mechanization of farming had led to stupendous increases in agricultural productivity. The wheat harvest soared from 152 million bushels in 1866 to 675 million bushels in 1900. Simultaneously, the price of a bushel of wheat fell from $1.53 to 58 cents. Unless they could afford the latest machinery, small family farms could not compete with large commercial farms. Beginning in the late 1880s and over the next decade, about 90 percent of all farms went bankrupt and sold out to larger establishments. People abandoned their farms and trekked to the cities to find work in the factories. The traditional influence of the farm on American society began its long decline.

RISE OF GOVERNMENT

The Industrial Revolution had brought undeniable benefits to vast numbers of people. On the other hand, it had also caused a widening gap between the rich and poor, unsafe and unhealthy factory working conditions, low pay and long hours, and environmental problems. Following the Civil War, America embarked on a long and continuing period of activist government to address those problems. Debate over the legitimate role of government was vigorous and often bitter. Frequently the legal arguments went all the way to the Supreme Court.

The people who moved to cities seeking factory jobs found cramped and run-down housing. A Providence, Rhode Island, yard.

Among the most important legislation that came from that debate was the Interstate Commerce Act of 1887. This act resulted from the power railroads possessed to set freight rates. Western and southern farmers complained to their congressmen that high, arbitrary freight rates were ruining them. A popular writer, Frank Norris, captured public opinion in his novel *The Octopus* when he described the railroads as "the

leviathan, with tentacles of steel clutching into the soil, the soulless Force, the iron-hearted power, the master, the Colossus, the Octopus." The Interstate Commerce Act regulated freight charges, setting the historic precedent that Congress could assume responsibility for managing a sector of the economy.

Another key act was the Sherman Antitrust Act of 1890. This legislation took aim at the ability of superrich

A New York basement apartment in the early years of the twentieth century.

industrialists such as John D. Rockefeller to destroy competition and maintain high prices by using the innovative form of business organization called the trust (see Volume 8). The Sherman Antitrust Act declared illegal "every contract, combination in the form of trust or otherwise, or conspiracy, in restraint of trade or commerce." Congress intended this language to end corporate monopolies.

CONSUMER CULTURE

The completion of the first transcontinental railroad (see Volume 8) created a truly national market. In theory, mass-produced goods could be sold to consumers everywhere. A number of businessmen tackled the challenge of making this theory a reality by developing an efficient system to distribute consumer goods. Among them was George H. Hartford. In 1860 Hartford began working for George F. Gilman's retail store, the Great American Tea Company, in New York City. Hartford and Gilman decided to expand the store to sell a variety of food products such as spices, milk, corn, and wheat. The store proved so successful that the partners opened several more stores in New York, all of them equally successful.

A notable feature of these stores was the owner's "cookie cutter" approach, with the stores having identical floor plans and products. Regardless of a store's location, a customer knew exactly where to find each product when he or she walked in the door. Such predictability made shoppers

Steel plant smokestacks polluting the air of an Alabama town during the early 1900s.

comfortable and, in turn, earned the stores loyal, repeat customers. By 1869 Gilman and Hartford owned ten stores and renamed them the Great Atlantic and Pacific Tea Company, or A&P.

A&P's success changed American retailing and caused other entrepreneurs to copy A&P's approach. Hartford's and Gilman's insight into customers' appreciation for comfortable routine led to chain-store retailing and the rise of an American consumer culture in which shopping became a leisure time, social activity.

CONCLUSION

The technological advances of the Industrial Revolution changed the face of society: how people worked, where they lived, how people and goods traveled from one place to another, and what people could buy. The new machines and technology also brought opportunity and material plenty to some, while consigning others to long hours of monotonous labor and an unending struggle to survive. The effort to balance the gains brought about by technological advancement with a fair and just society continues.

A&P pioneered the chain-store concept. An A&P store around 1900.

A DATELINE OF MAJOR EVENTS DURING THE INDUSTRIAL REVOLUTION

BEFORE 1750	1760	1770	1780

REVOLUTIONS IN INDUSTRY AND TECHNOLOGY

BEFORE 1750

1619: English settlers establish the first iron works in colonial America, near Jamestown, Virginia.

1689: Thomas Savery (England) patents the first design for a steam engine.

1709: Englishman Abraham Darby uses coke instead of coal to fuel his blast furnace.

1712: Englishman Thomas Newcomen builds the first working steam engine.

1717: Thomas Lombe establishes a silk-throwing factory in England.

1720: The first Newcomen steam engine on the Continent is installed at a Belgian coal mine.

1733: James Kay (England) invents the flying shuttle.

1742: Benjamin Huntsman begins making crucible steel in England.

1760

1756: The first American coal mine opens.

1764: In England James Hargreaves invents the spinning jenny.

1769: Englishman Richard Arkwright patents his spinning machine, called a water frame.

James Watt of Scotland patents an improved steam engine design.

Josiah Wedgwood (England) opens his Etruria pottery works.

1770

1771: An industrial spy smuggles drawings of the spinning jenny from England to France.

1774: John Wilkinson (England) builds machines for boring cannon cylinders.

1775: Arkwright patents carding, drawing, and roving machines.

In an attempt to end dependence on British textiles American revolutionaries open a spinning mill in Philadelphia using a smuggled spinning-jenny design.

1777: Oliver Evans (U.S.) invents a card-making machine.

1778: John Smeaton (England) introduces cast iron gearing to transfer power from waterwheels to machinery.

The water closet (indoor toilet) is invented in England.

1779: Englishman Samuel Crompton develops the spinning mule.

1780

1783: Englishman Thomas Bell invents a copper cylinder to print patterns on fabrics.

1784: Englishman Henry Cort invents improved rollers for rolling mills and the puddling process for refining pig iron.

Frenchman Claude Berthollet discovers that chlorine can be used as a bleach.

The ironworks at Le Creusot use France's first rotary steam engine to power its hammers, as well as using the Continent's first coke-fired blast furnace.

1785: Englishman Edmund Cartwright invents the power loom.

1788: The first steam engine is imported into Germany.

REVOLUTIONS IN TRANSPORTATION AND COMMUNICATION

1757: The first canal is built in England.

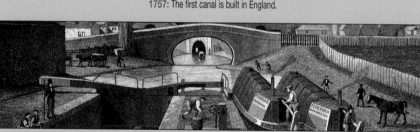

Locks on an English canal

1785: The first canal is built in the United States, at Richmond, Virginia.

1787: John Fitch and James Rumsey (U.S.) each succeed in launching a working steamboat.

SOCIAL REVOLUTIONS

1723: Britain passes an act to allow the establishment of workhouses for the poor.

1750: The enclosure of common land gains momentum in Britain.

1776: Scottish professor Adam Smith publishes *The Wealth of Nations*, which promotes laissez-faire capitalism.

The workhouse

INTERNATIONAL RELATIONS

Continental Army in winter quarters at Valley Forge

1775–1783: The American Revolution. Thirteen colonies win their independence from Great Britain and form a new nation, the United States of America.

1789–1793: The French Revolution leads to abolition of the monarchy and execution of the king and queen. Mass executions follow during the Reign of Terror, 1793–1794.

| **1790** | **1800** | **1810** | **1820** |

1790: English textile producer Samuel Slater begins setting up America's first successful textile factory in Pawtucket, Rhode Island.

Jacob Perkins (U.S.) invents a machine capable of mass-producing nails.

1791: French chemist Nicholas Leblanc invents a soda-making process.

1793: Eli Whitney (U.S.) invents a cotton gin.

1794: Germany's first coke-fired blast furnace is built.

The first German cotton spinning mill installs Arkwright's water frame.

1798: Eli Whitney devises a system for using power-driven machinery to produce interchangeable parts, the model for the "American System" of manufacture.

Wool-spinning mills are built in Belgium using machinery smuggled out of England.

A cylindrical papermaking machine is invented in England.

1801: American inventor Oliver Evans builds the first working high-pressure steam engine and uses it to power a mill.

Joseph-Marie Jacquard (France) invents a loom that uses punch cards to produce patterned fabrics.

A cotton-spinning factory based on British machinery opens in Belgium.

The first cotton-spinning mill in Switzerland begins operation.

Austria establishes the Continent's largest cotton-spinning mill.

1802: In England William Murdock uses coal gas to light an entire factory.

Richard Trevithick builds a high-pressure steam engine in England.

1807: British businessmen open an industrial complex in Belgium that includes machine manufacture, coal mining, and iron production.

1808: Russia's first spinning mill begins production in Moscow.

1810: Henry Maudslay (England) invents the precision lathe.

1816: Steam power is used for the first time in an American paper mill.

English scientist Humphry Davy invents a safety lamp for coal miners in England.

1817: The French iron industry's first puddling works and rolling mills are established.

1819: Thomas Blanchard (U.S.) invents a gunstock-turning lathe, which permits production of standardized parts.

A turning lathe

1821: Massachusetts businessmen begin developing Lowell as a site for textile mills.

1822: Power looms are introduced in French factories.

1820s: Spinning mills begin operation in Sweden.

Steam power is first used in Czech industry.

1827: A water-driven turbine is invented in France.

1794: The 66-mile Philadelphia and Lancaster turnpike begins operation.

Along an American Highway

1802: In England Richard Trevithick builds his first steam locomotive.

1807: Robert Fulton launches the Clermont, the first commercially successful steamboat, on the Hudson River in New York.

1811: Robert Fulton and his partner launch the first steamboat on the Mississippi River.

Construction begins on the Cumberland Road (later renamed the National Road) from Baltimore, Maryland, to Wheeling, Virginia.

1815: In England John McAdam develops an improved technique for surfacing roads.

1819: The first steamship crosses the Atlantic Ocean.

1825: The 363-mile Erie Canal is completed in America.

In England the first passenger railroad, the Stockton and Darlington Railway, begins operation.

1826: The 2-mile horse-drawn Granite Railroad in Massachusetts becomes the first American railroad.

1790: First American patent law passed.

Philadelphia begins building a public water system.

1798: Robert Owen takes over the New Lanark mills and begins implementing his progressive ideas.

1800: Parliament prohibits most labor union activity.

1802: Parliament passes a law limiting the working hours of poor children and orphans.

1811–1816: Luddite rioters destroy textile machinery in England.

1819: Parliament extends legal protection to all child laborers.

British cavalry fire at demonstrators demanding voting reform in Manchester, killing 11 and wounding hundreds, including women and children.

1827: Carpenters organize the first national trade union in Britain.

1799: Napoleon Bonaparte seizes control of France's government.

1792–1815: The Napoleonic Wars involve most of Europe, Great Britain, and Russia. France occupies many of its neighboring nations, reorganizes their governments, and changes their borders.

1812–1815: War between the United States and Great Britain disrupts America's foreign trade and spurs the development of American industry.

18th–century carpenter

A DATELINE OF MAJOR EVENTS DURING THE INDUSTRIAL REVOLUTION

	1830	1840	1850	1860
REVOLUTIONS IN INDUSTRY AND TECHNOLOGY	1830: Switzerland's first weaving mill established. 1831: British researcher Michael Faraday builds an electric generator. American inventor Cyrus McCormick builds a horse-drawn mechanical reaper. 1834: Bulgaria's first textile factory is built. 1835: Samuel Colt (U.S)invents the Colt revolver. The first steam engine is used to power a paper mill in Croatia. 1836: The first Hungarian steam mill, the Pest Rolling Mill company, begins using steam power to process grain. 1837: The first successful coke-fired blast furnace in the United States begins operation.	American blacksmith John Deere introduces the first steel plow. 1842: Britain lifts restrictions on exporting textile machinery.	1849: The California Gold Rush begins. 1850: Swedish sawmills begin using steam power. 1851: The Great Exhibition opens at the Crystal Palace in London. William Kelly of Kentucky invents a process for converting pig iron to steel. 1852: Hydraulic mining is introduced in the American West. 1853: The first cotton-spinning mill opens in India. 1856: William Perkin (England) synthesizes the first coal tar dye. Henry Bessemer (England) announces his process for converting pig iron to steel. Isaac Singer (U.S.) introduces the sewing machine.	1859: Edwin Drake successfully drills for oil in Pennsylvania. 1863: Ernest Solvay of Belgium begins working on a process to recover ammonia from soda ash in order to produce bleaching powder. 1864: Switzerland's first major chemical company is established. The Siemens-Martin open-hearth steelmaking process is perfected in France. 1865: The first oil pipeline opens in America. The rotary web press is invented in America, permitting printing on both sides of the paper. 1866: U.S. government surveyors discover the largest-known deposit of iron ore in the world in the Mesabi Range of northern Minnesota.

Making Bessemer steel

	1830	1840	1850	1860
REVOLUTIONS IN TRANSPORTATION AND COMMUNICATION	1830: The first locomotive-powered railroad to offer regular service begins operating in South Carolina. The opening of the Liverpool and Manchester Railway marks the beginning of the British railroad boom. 1833: The 60-mile Camden and Amboy Railroad of New Jersey is completed. 1835: Construction begins on Germany's first railroad.	1836: First railroad built in Russia. 1843: Tunnel completed under the Thames River, London, England, the world's first to be bored through soft clay under a riverbed. 1844: Samuel Morse (U.S.) sends the first message via his invention, the telegraph. The nation's first steam-powered sawmill begins operation on the West Coast.	1846: First railroad built in Hungary. 1853: The first railway is completed in India. 1854: Americans complete the Moscow-St. Petersburg railroad line. 1855: Switzerland's first railroad opens.	1859: In France Etienne Lenoir invents an internal combustion engine. 1860–1861: The Pony Express, a system of relay riders, carries mail to and from America's West Coast. 1866: The transatlantic telegraph cable is completed. Congress authorizes construction of a transcontinental telegraph line. 1869: The tracks of two railroad companies meet at Promontory, Utah, to complete America's first transcontinental railroad

	1830	1840	1850	1860
SOCIAL REVOLUTIONS	1833: Parliament passes the Factory Act to protect children working in textile factories. 1836–1842: The English Chartist movement demands Parliamentary reform, but its petitions are rejected by Parliament. 1838: The U.S. Congress passes a law regulating steamboat boiler safety, the first attempt by the federal government to regulate private behavior in the interest of public safety.	1842: Parliament bans the employment of children and women underground in mines. 1845: Russia bans strikes. 1847: A new British Factory Act limits working hours to 10 hours a day or 58 hours a week for children aged 13 to 18 and for women. 1848: Marx and Engels coauthor the Communist Manifesto.	1854: In England Charles Dickens publishes *Hard Times*, a novel based on his childhood as a factory worker. 1857: Brooklyn, New York, builds a city wastewater system.	1860–1910: More than 20 million Europeans emigrate to the United States. 1866: National Labor Union forms in the United States. 1869: Knights of Labor forms in the United States. Founding of the Great Atlantic and Pacific Tea Company (A&P) in the U.S.

	1830	1840	1850	1860
INTERNATIONAL RELATIONS	1839–1842: Great Britain defeats China in a war and forces it to open several ports to trade.	1847: Austro-Hungary occupies Italy. 1848: Failed revolutions take place in France, Germany, and Austro-Hungary. Serfdom ends in Austro-Hungary.	1853: The American naval officer Commodore Matthew Perry arrives in Japan. 1853–1856: France, Britain, and Turkey defeat Russia in the Crimean War. 1858: Great Britain takes control of India, retaining it until 1947.	1861–1865: The American Civil War brings about the end of slavery in the United States and disrupts raw cotton supplies for U.S. and foreign cotton mills. 1867: Britain gains control of parts of Malaysia. Malaysia is a British colony from 1890 to 1957.

1870	1880	1890	1900

1860s: Agricultural machinery introduced in Hungary.

1870: John D. Rockefeller establishes the Standard Oil Company (U.S.).

1873: The Bethlehem Steel Company begins operation in Pennsylvania.

1875: The first modern iron and steel works opens in India.

Investment in the Japan's cotton industry booms.

1876: Philadelphia hosts the Centennial Exposition.

1877: Hungary installs its first electrical system.

1879: Charles Brush builds the nation's first arc-lighting system in San Francisco.

Thomas Edison (U.S.) develops the first practical incandescent light bulb.

1870s: Japan introduces mechanical silk-reeling.

1882: In New York City the Edison Electric Illuminating Company begins operating the world's first centralized electrical generating station.

1884: The U.S. Circuit Court bans hydraulic mining.

George Westinghouse (U.S.) founds Westinghouse Electric Company.

English engineer Charles Parsons develops a steam turbine.

1885: The introduction of band saws makes American lumbering more efficient.

German inventor Carl Benz builds a self-propelled vehicle powered by a single cylinder gas engine with electric ignition.

1887: An English power plant is the first to use steam turbines to generate electricity.

1888: Nikola Tesla (U.S.) invents an alternating current electric motor.

1894: An American cotton mill becomes the first factory ever built to rely entirely on electric power.

1895: George Westinghouse builds the world's first generating plant designed to transmit power over longer distances—a hydroelectric plant at Niagara Falls to transmit alternating current some 20 miles to consumers in Buffalo, New York.

1901: The United States Steel Corporation is formed by a merger of several American companies.

Japan opens its first major iron and steel works.

1929: The U.S.S.R. begins implementing its first Five-Year Plan, which places nationwide industrial development under central government control.

Power generators at Edison Electric

1875: Japan builds its first railway.

1876: In the U.S. Alexander Graham Bell invents the telephone.

German inventor Nikolaus Otto produces a practical gasoline engine.

1870s: Sweden's railroad boom.

1883: Brooklyn Bridge completed.

1885: Germans Gottlieb Daimler and Wilhelm Maybach build the world's first motorcycle.

1886: Daimler and Maybach invent the carburetor, the device that efficiently mixes fuel and air in internal combustion engines

1888: The first electric urban streetcar system begins operation in Richmond, Virginia.

1893: American brothers Charles and J. Frank Duryea build a working gasoline-powered automobile.

1896: Henry Ford builds a demonstration car powered by an internal combustion engine.

1896–1904: Russia builds the Manchurian railway in China.

1903: Henry Ford establishes Ford Motor Company.

1904: New York City subway system opens.

Trans-Siberian Railroad completed.

1908: William Durant, maker of horse-drawn carriages, forms the General Motors Company.

1909: Ford introduces the Model T automobile.

1870: Parliament passes a law to provide free schooling for poor children.

1872: France bans the International Working Men's Association.

1874: France applies its child labor laws to all industrial establishments and provides for inspectors to enforce the laws.

1877: Wage cuts set off the Great Railroad Strike in West Virginia, and the strike spreads across the country. Federal troops kill 35 strikers.

1880: Parliament makes school attendance compulsory for children between the ages of 5 and 10.

1881: India passes a factory law limiting child employment.

1884: Germany passes a law requiring employers to provide insurance against workplace accidents.

1886: American Federation of Labor forms.

1887: U.S. Interstate Commerce Act passed to regulate railroad freight charges.

1890: The U.S. government outlaws monopolies with passage of the Sherman Antitrust Act.

1892: Workers strike at Carnegie Steel in Homestead, Pennsylvania, in response to wage cuts. An armed confrontation results in 12 deaths.

1894: The Pullman strike, called in response to wage cuts, halts American railroad traffic. A confrontation with 2,000 federal troops kills 12 strikers in Chicago.

1900: Japan passes a law to limit union activity.

1902: The United Mine Workers calls a nationwide strike against coal mines, demanding eight-hour workdays and higher wages.

1903: Socialists organize the Russian Social Democratic Workers Party.

1931: Japan passes a law to limit working hours for women and children in textile factories.

1870: The city-states of Italy unify to form one nation.

1871: Parisians declare self-government in the city but are defeated by government forces.

Prussia and the other German states unify to form the German Empire.

1877–1878: War between Russia and Turkey. Bulgaria gains independence from Turkey.

1900–1901: A popular uprising supported by the Chinese government seeks to eject all foreigners from China.

1917: Russian Revolution

1929: A worldwide economic depression begins.

AMERICAN INDUSTRIALISTS

ANDREW CARNEGIE: 1835–1919; born in Scotland. Andrew Carnegie's father was a hand-loom weaver who lost his livelihood to industrialization. The family emigrated to the United States and arrived at a town near Pittsburgh, Pennsylvania, in 1848. Through hard work, education, saving, careful investment, and innovative thinking Carnegie advanced from a teenage cotton mill employee to a major industrialist and possibly the wealthiest man of his era. After selling his steel company, he donated large sums to fund a university, a school for blacks, and pensions for workers. (See Volume 8 for more about Carnegie.)

HENRY FRICK: 1849–1919; born in Pennsylvania. The young Frick found school boring and dropped out to work for his father's whiskey distillery. He decided that he could make a fortune in the steel industry, so he invested his savings in building coke ovens. By the time he was 30 years old, Frick had made millions of dollars and owned more than a thousand coke ovens. Andrew Carnegie bought Frick's company in 1882 and hired Frick to work for him. Frick did much to make Carnegie Steel successful, but his handling of the Homestead strike (see page 36 of this volume) caused a rupture between the two men. Frick later joined forces with J.P. Morgan to found United States Steel Corporation.

GEORGE PULLMAN: 1831–1897; born in New York. Pullman quit school at the age of 14 and apprenticed himself to a cabinetmaker. He gained a reputation for his skill, moved to Chicago in 1855 to start his own construction company, and worked at remodeling railroad cars. Dissatisfied with business, he left Chicago and opened general stores in several Colorado mining towns, but decided to return to Chicago after a few years. His 1864 railroad sleeping car design became popular and launched him on the path to wealth. Pullman's name became associated with luxurious railroad cars, but the 1894 strike against his company (see pages 36, 39–40) exposed his unfair labor practices and destroyed his reputation.

FOUNDERS OF THE AMERICAN LABOR MOVEMENT

EUGENE DEBS: 1855–1926; born in Indiana. Eugene Debs's career path led from school dropout to locomotive fireman, union organizer, state legislator, prisoner, and presidential candidate. Debs founded the American Railway Union, which grew to have one of the largest memberships in the United States, and the Socialist Party of America. (See pages 42-43 of this volume for more about Debs.)

SAMUEL GOMPERS: 1850–1924; born in London, England. At the age of 13 Samuel Gompers left England for America and took a job rolling cigars, which was also his father's trade. He soon joined the cigar-maker's union and took a leadership role. Gompers became an American citizen in 1872 and disapproved of the socialism that other labor leaders supported. Gompers was president of the American Federation of Labor from 1886 to 1894 and, after a brief takeover by socialists, again from 1895 until 1924.

MARY HARRIS "MOTHER" JONES: 1830–1930; born in Ireland. After emigrating to Canada and spending her childhood there, Jones moved to Tennessee, worked as a schoolteacher and dressmaker, married, and had four children. Her husband and all her children died in a yellow fever epidemic in 1867. She became devoted to the labor movement when a union office took her in after she lost her home in the Chicago fire. She helped establish the International Workers of the World in 1905. (See page 38 of this volume for more about Jones.)

TERENCE POWDERLY: 1849–1924; born in Pennsylvania to Irish immigrants. Powderly went to work for the railroad at the age of 13 and later apprenticed himself to a railroad machinist. He entered politics to promote the interests of labor, was elected mayor of Scranton, Pennsylvania, and served three terms from 1878 to 1884. In 1879 Powderly also became "grand master" of the Knights of Labor, a once-secret labor organization that had just given up its secrecy. He relinquished leadership in 1893 when socialists took over the organization. Powderly then worked as an attorney. (See pages 28–29 of this volume for more about Powderly.)

WILLIAM SYLVIS: 1828–1870; born in Pennsylvania. Sylvis quit school at the age of 14 and became an apprentice molder in an iron foundry. He tried unsuccessfully to start his own business before entering labor union politics. After founding the National Labor Union, Sylvis turned it into a political party to promote the interests of workers and ran unsuccessfully for president of the United States.

GLOSSARY

APPRENTICE: young person in training for a skilled trade, bound by an agreement with a master of the trade

ARTISANS: skilled craftsmen who worked in such trades as shoemaking, printing, or making cutlery

BOYCOTT: an agreement to refuse to buy from or sell to certain businesses

CAPITALISM: the economic system in which property and businesses are privately owned and operated for personal profit

CAPITALIST: a person who invests money in a business

CESSPOOL: a pit to receive and store household wastewater and sewage

CORPORATION: a legally constituted business with the right to buy and sell, lend and borrow, and sue and be sued

COTTAGE INDUSTRY: manufacturing goods at home

DEPRESSION: decrease in business activity accompanied by unemployment and lower prices and earnings

ENTREPRENEUR: one who establishes and manages a business

FACTORY DISCIPLINE: the requirements of factory employment, including adherence to the factory work schedule and keeping pace with the machines

FIXED COSTS: the cost of the buildings and permanent equipment needed to operate a business

GUILD: medieval form of trade association, whereby skilled workers in the same craft or trade organized to protect their business interests

INJUNCTION: a court order issued to prohibit a specific activity

JOURNEYMEN: skilled workers who have learned their trade by completing an apprenticeship or other form of training

MUCKRAKERS: term coined by Theodore Roosevelt to describe newspaper reporters who search for and publish evidence of corruption among politicians and business owners

RADICAL: extreme; holding extreme views; one who favors major changes to the social order

ROBBER BARON: name given by journalists to extraordinarily wealthy, aggressive, unscrupulous, and successful American businessmen of the nineteenth century

SCRIP: pieces of paper used in place of money

SOCIALISM: an economic system in which the community owns all property and operates all businesses with the aim of sharing the work and profits equally; communists viewed socialism as an intermediate stage in the evolution from capitalism to communism.

SOLIDARITY: unity of belief or action

STORM SEWERS: underground pipes to collect rainwater and carry it away from city streets

STRIKE: a collective refusal to work until an employer agrees to meet employee demands

TENEMENT: a building divided into numerous small apartments, often overcrowded or in poor condition

TRUST: an arrangement in which stockholders give a board of trustees a controlling interest in their company and receive trust certificates in return

UNION: association of workers for the purpose of obtaining better wages and working conditions

ADDITIONAL RESOURCES

BOOKS:

Bartoletti, Susan Campbell. *Kids on Strike!* Boston: Houghton Mifflin, 2003.

Dunwell, Steve. *The Run of the Mill.* Boston: David R. Godine, 1978.

Gourley, Catherine. *Good Girl Work: Factories, Sweatshops, and How Women Changed Their Role in the American Workforce.* Brookfield, CT: Millbrook Press, 1999.

Jones, Mother. *The Autobiography of Mother Jones.* Chicago: Charles H. Kerr, 1990.

Olson, James S. *Encyclopedia of the Industrial Revolution in America.* Westport, CT: Greenwood Press, 2002.

Richards, John Stuart. *Early Coal Mining in the Anthracite Region.* Charleston, SC: Arcadia Publishing, 2002.

WEBSITES

http://www.americaslibrary.gov
Select "Jump Back in Time"

http://www.cis.yale.edu/amstud/inforev/riis/title.html
Reproduction of an 1890 illustrated book, *How the Other Half Lives*, about life in New York tenements

http://www.eugenevdebs.com/
Official website of the Eugene V. Debs Foundation, with information resources about his life and work

http://historymatters.gmu.edu
Type in the search term "Industrial Revolution" for articles about the labor movement

http://www.historyplace.com/unitedstates/childlabor/index.html
Photos by Lewis Hine of child laborers in the United States, 1908-1912

http://www.ilr.cornell.edu/trianglefire/
Story and images of the 1911 Triangle Shirtwaist Factory fire in New York City, in which 146 employees died

http://pbskids.org/wayback/tech1900/
About technology in America in 1900

SET INDEX